—P E O P L E T O K N O W—

AL GORE

United States Vice President

Betty Burford

ENSLOW PUBLISHERS, INC.

Bloy St. & Ramsey Ave.	P.O. Box 38
Box 777	Aldershot
Hillside, N.J. 07205	Hants GU12 6BP
U.S.A.	U.K.

Library of Congress Cataloging-in-Publication Data

Burford, Betty
    Al Gore: United States vice president / Betty Burford.
        p. cm. — (People to know)
    Includes bibliographical references (p.) and index.
    ISBN 0-89490-496-5
    1. Gore, Albert, 1948– —Juvenile literature. 2. Vice-Presidents—
United States—Biography—Juvenile literature.
[1. Gore, Albert, 1948– . 2. Vice-Presidents.] I. Title. II. Series.
E840.8.G65B86   1994
973.929'092—dc20   93-47475
[B]   CIP
                                   AC

Printed in the United States of America

10 9 8 7 6 5 4 3 2 1

Contents

Albert Gore, Jr.

1

The 1992 Democratic National Convention

On the night of July 16, 1992, Madison Square Garden in New York City seemed alive with excitement. The delegates to the Democratic National Convention had gathered on the meeting's last night to hear the acceptance speeches of their two candidates: William Jefferson Clinton for President and Albert Gore, Jr., for Vice President. For four days the work of the convention had gone forward smoothly. The party platform—the positions on social and political issues that the party would support—had been agreed upon. Keynote speeches and nominating speeches had also been delivered. Now, at last—amid the raucous music, the balloons, the bunting, and the swooping spotlights—the delegates on the convention floor waited in eager anticipation.

Each delegation, made up of important state and local politicians, sat in a group under a banner with its state's name on it. Prominently placed near the podium were the banners of Arkansas and Tennessee. Bill Clinton from Arkansas would make the final speech of the evening. But first the huge crowd was impatient to hear from Clinton's choice for Vice President—Senator Al Gore from Tennessee.

Sitting in one of the many box seats ringing the huge arena were Al Gore's family: his wife Tipper and their children—Karenna, Kristin, Sarah, and Albert III. Gore's mother Pauline and father Albert Gore, Sr. were also seated in the box. Al Gore, Sr. was very familiar with the convention scene. He had been in political life as a member of the U.S. Congress for thirty-two years.

When Al Gore came to the podium to make his speech, he was greeted by wild cheering and applause, punctuated by whistles and horn blasts. At last the crowd quieted and sat back to listen. The eyes of everyone in the vast hall were on the lone figure at the podium. After an introductory joke, Gore immediately became serious.

In positive and ringing tones he said loudly and firmly, "My friends, I thank you for your confidence . . . I pledge to pour my heart and soul into this crusade on behalf of the American people." (And here his tone became, if possible, even more resolute), "I accept your nomination for the Vice-Presidency of the United States of America."[1] Gore went on to talk about recent changes in the world: the tearing down of the Berlin Wall, the end of the Cold War, the end of communist rule in Eastern Europe, and the coming end to the racial separation, called apartheid, in South Africa.

This speech would prove to be one of the best of Al Gore's career thus far. He warmed to his task as he criticized the then current Bush-Quayle Administration. There is a popular technique in political speechmaking in which speechmakers get the audience to recite a refrain on cue. Gore used that technique as he made specific his criticisms of George Bush and Dan Quayle.

"They have given us false choices, bad choices, and no choice. And it is time for them to go."[2] In short paragraphs he made charge after charge against the Administration, ending each with the soon familiar phrase "It is time for them to go." Finally he was able to say, "They have demeaned our democracy with the politics of distraction, denial, and despair. What time is it?" And, of course, the crowd was ready. They eagerly chanted at the top of their lungs, "It is time for them to go!"

In his speech Al Gore spoke of Bill Clinton's

considerable achievements as governor of Arkansas. Then he turned to his own concerns:

> I've spent much of my career working to protect the environment, not only because it is vital to the future of my state of Tennessee, our country, and our earth air, but because I believe there is a fundamental link between our current relationship to the earth and the attitudes that stand in the way of human progress.[3]

As Gore addressed the question of racial strife in America he said:

> We have another challenge as well. In the wake of the Cold War and in the reemergence of ancient ethnic and racial hatreds throughout the world, the United States must once again prove that there is a better way . . .[4]

Bill Clinton's choice of Al Gore had surprised many people. Usually presidential nominees choose someone different from themselves in order to strengthen the party ticket. Al Gore was very much like Bill Clinton: they were both young and of the same generation—only nineteen months apart in age. They also came from the same geographic region, southern states adjacent to each other, rather than from different parts of the country. As Gore finished speaking, to thunderous applause, it was clear that the convention delegates were delighted with Clinton's choice.

The coming campaign was far from a sure bet. But the mood of the wildly cheering delegates on the floor of Madison Square Garden that July night was totally positive. The delegates sensed victory in the 1992 election. Bill Clinton would be the next President of the United States, and Al Gore would win a job for which his entire political career had prepared him—the forty-fifth Vice President of the United States of America.

Like Father, Like Son

The family into which Albert Arnold Gore, Jr. was born on March 31, 1948, was a highly political one. His father Albert Gore, Sr. was serving his fifth term in the U.S. House of Representatives, representing Tennessee's Fourth Congressional District. His mother Pauline Gore worked side by side with her husband in his congressional office. As a representative, Albert Gore, Sr. always studied any legislative question extensively. When he went on the floor of the House of Representatives to debate or make a speech, he was always thoroughly prepared.

Al, Jr. was the couple's second child. Their first child, daughter Nancy, was ten years old when Al, Jr. was born. Albert, Sr. had made no secret about wishing for a boy this second time. He got the editor of a leading

Nashville newspaper, *The Tennessean*, to agree that if the child was a boy he would run the story of his birth on page one. The editor kept his word, and on April 1, *The Tennessean* proclaimed, "A son was born to Mrs. Pauline Gore in Washington yesterday and *The Tennessean* hereby makes good on a long-standing promise to Representative Albert Gore to give this good news page-one play."[1]

The Gores had lived in Tennessee for generations. One Gore ancestor had fought in the American Revolution and had been given a grant of land in Overton County, Tennessee. Albert Gore, Sr. was born on a farm near Carthage, Tennessee. He met his future wife Pauline LaFon in the coffee shop of the Andrew Jackson Hotel in Nashville, where she was a waitress.

LaFon was working her way through law school while Gore was studying part-time toward his law degree. It was unusual for a woman to study for a profession in the early 1930s. In fact, when she received her diploma, Pauline LaFon was the only woman in her graduating class and one of the few women graduates of Vanderbilt University Law School. After graduation she practiced law for a year before marrying Albert Gore. Then she gave up her profession to devote herself to Gore's career and raising a family.

President Franklin Roosevelt's Secretary of State Cordell Hull—considered Carthage's foremost citizen—was the man who got Albert Gore, Sr. into politics. Gore

The Gore family used a jeep to ride around their farm near Carthage, Tennessee. Nancy, Al, Jr.'s sister, was ten years older than him and old enough to drive while he was still a little boy.

admired Hull immensely and wanted to follow in his footsteps as congressperson from Tennessee's Fourth District. Gore's problem was that he had no money for a campaign in 1938. He mortgaged the family farm at Carthage to raise funds. Then he began visiting his district with a hillbilly band that played country music. Gore was an accomplished fiddler himself and played with the band while campaigning for votes as often as ten to fifteen times a day. When the election results were tallied, Albert Gore, Sr. was the winner. In coming years he would be reelected to the House of Representatives six more times.

Gore became more and more influential in Congress as time passed. In 1947—a year before Al, Jr. was born—he was honored by the Democratic leadership of the House of Representatives by being chosen as one of their party's select watchdog team. Six Democrats were supposed to observe the Republican opposition and spotlight any mistakes.

Both Representative and Mrs. Gore were strong supporters of President Franklin Roosevelt. Coming from backgrounds of farms and small towns, they felt grateful for programs such as the Rural Electrification Act. This legislation had brought electricity to the farms of America. In later years Gore was one of the first southerners in Congress to vote for civil rights legislation. He refused to sign the Southern Manifesto, which required all southern congresspersons to declare their opposition to the Supreme Court's decision (*Brown v. the Board of Education,* 1954) to desegregate public schools. Al Gore, Sr. became one of the most powerful and influential members of Congress.

The Gores were also one of the most popular couples in Washington, D.C., society. Once as Albert, Sr. and Pauline were leaving for a formal evening, Al, Jr. said to his father, "Dad, save that outfit. I might need it someday."[2] The son was referring to his father's white tie and tails.

Except in the summer, when Congress was not in session, the Gore family lived in an apartment in Washington, D.C., in the Fairfax Hotel (now called the Ritz-Carlton). The old Fairfax was far from luxurious in the years the Gores lived there; it was even somewhat plain. The hotel is surrounded by foreign embassies. In nice weather the Gore family would take walks down Massachusetts Avenue. The adults played a game with the children that involved guessing the identity of an embassy from the flag flying over it.

During the summer the Gore family returned to the farm at Carthage. There they raised corn and tobacco and kept a herd of cattle. The town of Carthage is typical of many small towns all across America at that time. Old men often sat on the courthouse steps whittling. And the beauty parlor, called "Kaye's Clip and Curl," circulated local news.

When staying on the farm, the Gore family attended

Watched by little Al, Jr., his father replaced a string on his fiddle. Albert Gore, Sr. was an accomplished fiddler. He campaigned with a hillbilly band, but he gave it up when Mrs. Gore said she thought it was not dignified.

the New Salem Missionary Baptist Church. The simple one-room church is situated up the road from the Gores' farm, in between a one-truck fire station and a cornfield.

Albert Gore, Sr. ultimately went on to become a senator from Tennessee, a position in which he served with distinction for eighteen years. As a senator, one of his finest achievements was the massive federal highway building program which he supported. In order to keep his constituents informed about the work of Congress, he prepared radio programs for stations in middle Tennessee. In this way he was taking a leaf from the book of President Roosevelt, who made informal radio broadcasts, called "fireside chats," to the nation.

Albert Gore, Sr. was known in Congress as being frank and outspoken; he was viewed as an independent thinker and a hard worker who always did his homework. In time, his son would come to be known in the U.S. Congress for these same qualities. But that lay in the future. First, Al Gore, Jr. had some growing up to do.

Two Separate Lives

Al Gore, Jr. lived two very different lives as he was growing up. During the winter months he stayed with his parents in an apartment in the Fairfax Hotel. During the summer and holidays Al moved to the Gore's 250-acre farm outside the little town of Carthage, Tennessee.

Senator and Mrs. Gore led very busy lives which required travel, so Al often stayed with the farm's caretaker William Thompson and his wife Alota. At first the Thompson's tenant house didn't have any indoor plumbing, though later the house was remodeled and plumbing was installed. Al was a great friend of the Thompson's son Gordon, who was the same age as Al. The two boys worked and played together.

They often played with Gorden's dog, Patsy. Once

Al and Gordon made a harness for Patsy so they could hitch her up to a wagon and get her to pull them around the yard. One day Patsy was nowhere to be found, and Mrs. Thompson was sure the dog was gone for good. Al, however, insisted that they would find Patsy and he looked for her tirelessly. After a few days he and Gordon located Patsy in a corn crib—somehow the dog had gotten into the crib and then couldn't get out.

Life on the Carthage farm was great fun for children. There were horses and cattle as well as the Caney Fork River for swimming, fishing, and canoeing.

When Al was seven years old, the Popes came to live on the farm. Mr. Pope worked on the farm raising crops and taking care of the livestock. His son Terry was about Al's age, and the two boys became fast friends. Al had a collie dog named Buff. When Buff had puppies, Al gave a pup to Terry. Terry's pup, Lady, grew into a beautiful dog. The two boys argued as to which dog—Buff or Lady—was better looking. They decided to get Mrs. Gore to be the judge. Somehow Pauline Gore answered this sensitive question so diplomatically that each boy thought she had chosen his dog. When Al was eight years old his father gave him what most children that age would want for Christmas—a pony.

Both Al and Terry were strong and avid swimmers. At first they swam in the river. But after a swimming pool was built in Carthage, they swam there as well.

Life was not all play, however. Al's father believed in

The Gores enjoyed boating on the Caney Fork River. The river ran through their 250-acre farm.

hard work.[1] Al, Jr. had jobs to do on the farm such as cutting tobacco or hauling hay. Al, Sr. was a strict disciplinarian too. He raised his son to be polite, respectful, and considerate of other people.

When he was young, Al, Jr. attended the elementary school in Carthage until fourth grade. From the start he was a very good and serious student. His second-grade teacher Eleanor Smotherman said about Al, "When I talked with him, I almost had to look at him to see whether I was talking to a child or an adult."[2]

Al started at the St. Albans School for Boys in Washington, D.C., when he entered fourth grade. There he studied the usual reading, writing, and arithmetic—plus history, science, foreign languages, religion, art, and music. Though Al seemed to like St. Albans, his fourth-grade teacher thought that Al really wanted to be back in Carthage. After all, that's where his dog and pony were. In a newspaper interview years later, Gore confirmed that he, indeed, preferred Carthage. "I'm happy that my parents gave me a good education . . . but if you're a boy and you have the choice between the eighth floor of a hotel and a big farm with horses, cows, canoes, and a river, it was an easy choice for me."[3]

During his high school years at St. Albans, Al's subjects were pretty much the same as they had been. He was also allowed to take some extracurricular courses—usually choosing courses in painting and creative writing. Al managed to make excellent grades

St. Albans, where Al Gore went to school in Washington, D.C., is one of America's most prestigious prep schools. Al started St. Albans beginning with fourth grade.

while at the same time being very involved in athletics. From his earliest years at St. Albans, whenever it was permitted, he bounced a basketball. He must have followed this practice at home as well because his apartment neighbors complained. In high school Al won his varsity letter in football, basketball, and track. In his senior year he was also captain of the football team.

When Al, Jr. was fourteen he invited the sister of a friend to go to a drive-in movie with him. Donna Armistead was nearly sixteen at the time and had some hesitation about dating a boy two years younger than she was.[4] The two decided to make it a double date with Donna's brother Roy and his girlfriend. Instead of watching the movie, Al and Donna sat in the back seat and talked nonstop for two hours about all sorts of subjects—school, Carthage, friends, the future. The next day Al asked Donna to be his girlfriend and to go steady with him, and she agreed. While Al was away at school in Washington he wrote Donna every day—and sometimes twice a day. He also called her faithfully every Saturday night at 7:30.

The Gores liked Donna, and she was always more than welcome at the family farm. Al quickly became like one of the family at Donna's home as well. He participated in all Armistead family doings.

Al and the close-knit group of friends he had in Carthage worked and played together. One of their gathering places was the New Salem Missionary Baptist Church, which was something of a center of social life. Another place where the group gathered was the B & B Drive In on Highway 70. A typical summer day for Al Gore might have passed in the following way: working in the cornfields in the morning, cutting tobacco in the afternoon, then meeting friends at the river to swim, and finally off to the B & B for burgers and a soda.

At summer's end Al would leave the farm and return to school. He kept the two halves of his life completely separate. He never invited Donna to visit at St. Albans and he said very little to his Carthage friends about that part of his life. Conversely, he didn't talk to his school friends in Washington about his Carthage friends and life on the farm in Tennessee.

Al's time in the nation's capital was full and interesting. Washington, D.C., is a city filled with cultural opportunities. And Al Gore took advantage of the chance to visit such places as the Smithsonian Institution and the National Gallery.

He was also very active in the extracurricular activities at St. Albans. Al was class treasurer for two years and served on the student council. Showing an early interest in politics, he was made Liberal Party Leader in his senior year.

In each issue of the St. Albans' yearbook, the editor wrote a brief comment about each graduating student,

A serious Al Gore posed for his high school yearbook picture. The yearbook said that it would probably not be long before Gore reached the top. It was an accurate prediction.

which appeared under his picture. In the 1965 yearbook under Al Gore's picture the editor commented:

> Al is frighteningly good at many things. Varsity football Captain, basketball and track standout, Liberal Party Leader in Government Class, scholar, artist extraordinary, Al has stood out in many fields of endeavor. Popular and respected he would seem the epitome of the all-American Young Man. It probably won't be long before Al reaches the top. When he does, all of his classmates will remark to themselves, "I knew that guy was going somewhere in life."[5]

Al Gore was looking forward to the traditional graduation dance, but he had no idea how important that event would be for him. It was at this dance that he was introduced to a beautiful, blonde, young woman from Virginia. Her name was Mary Elizabeth Aitcheson, but she went by the childhood nickname of "Tipper." Al Gore had met his future wife. Very soon Al and Tipper were spending every available minute together. That summer Al Gore and Donna broke up, and a year later Donna got married to someone else.

As his senior year drew to a close, Gore was elated by the crowning achievement of his high school career: he was a National Merit Scholarship Finalist. Al Gore was admitted to the college of his choice. It was Harvard University.

College and the Draft

Early in his freshman year at Harvard, John Tyson heard a knock on the door of his dormitory room. He went and opened the door. Standing in the doorway was a tall, good-looking, young man. "Hi," he said with a slight Southern drawl. "I'm Al Gore. I'm running for freshman council."[1] This meeting was the beginning of a long and close friendship between Gore and the burly African-American football player. John Tyson not only voted for Al Gore, but also became his roommate.

Gore and Tyson lived in a dormitory called Dunster House. They shared a living room which had a fireplace and a window with a view of the Charles River. Their bedroom was furnished with bunk beds. The roommates divided the time each had the lower bunk. Half the time Gore slept below, and half the time Tyson did. "You really get to know a guy when you share bunk beds with him," John Tyson noted.[2]

College studies left no time for such hobbies as painting, but Al Gore continued to participate in sports. He played football, and more notably, basketball for his house. He was very competitive in a friendly sort of way. Gore was what is known as a shooting guard, possessing a ferocious eighteen-foot jump shot. He was also renowned for his tenacious defense.

Frisbees were all the rage at that time, and Gore and Tyson spent fun times throwing a Frisbee on the bank of the Charles River.[3] They also found time to indulge in handball to the point where their hands became calloused.

Gore was known at Harvard as the guy with the motorcycle, which he rode everywhere. Tyson was impressed with the way Gore thought nothing of picking up Tyson's sister at the airport when she came to see her brother play football.[4] Al would put Tyson's sister on the back of his motorcycle and ride straight through downtown Boston. One has to remember that this was in the late 1960s, when it was unusual to see a white man with a black woman. Also, many people were prejudiced against such sights.

Gore and Tipper corresponded during her senior year in high school. They agreed that she should choose a college in Boston so that they could be near each other. After choosing Garland College, a junior college in

Boston, and graduating there *cum laude,* she enrolled in Boston University and majored in child psychology.

Al Gore, not surprisingly, majored in American government. He had the advantage of learning about his major via tutorials. He was taught in a one-on-one situation with people who were authorities on his special interest—the American presidency. His senior thesis was titled "The Impact of Television on the Conduct of the Presidency, 1947–1969." It dealt in detail with presidential debates.

Gore made good use of the summer breaks to gain varied job experiences. One year he worked in Brussels, Belgium, and another in Mexico City where he became fluent in Spanish. His love of his native state led him to study Tennessee history at Memphis State University. He spent another summer working as a copyboy at *The New York Times.*

In March 1966 Al Gore turned eighteen. He obeyed the law and returned to Tennessee to register for the draft. He realized that as a student he would be deferred and would not have to serve in the armed forces until after he graduated.

During this time the Vietnam War was dividing Americans. The United States had more or less drifted into what became the longest war in American history, lasting from 1965 until 1973—when U.S. forces finally left the country. Though Vietnam had long been a French colony, it was occupied by the Japanese during

World War II. At the end of the war an international peace conference divided the country in two. The north was in the hands of the communists while the south was governed by non-communists.

After Japan's defeat, France tried to regain control of Vietnam. It fought against the Vietminh, as the communists were called, for eight long years. Finally in 1954 the French suffered a terrible defeat at a place called Dienbienphu and gave up the struggle.

When the leader of South Vietnam would not hold elections to reunify the country, the Vietminh in the south began to rebel. After 1957 these rebels, who came to be called Vietcong (VC), received increasing support from North Vietnam. Later China and the Soviet Union aided North Vietnam in its struggle to take control of the entire country.

The United States had committed itself to helping any free country that was menaced by communism. So the U.S. government began sending observers to South Vietnam. By 1965 President Lyndon B. Johnson believed that he had to send in American ground forces to defend U.S. air bases and to prevent the North Vietnamese and the Vietcong from taking over South Vietnam. As the war escalated, American troops were sent to Vietnam. Soon U.S. forces began to bomb North Vietnam.

U.S. citizens became split into "hawks," who supported the war, and "doves," who felt that Americans had no business fighting a war in Asia when U.S. safety was not at stake. TV news reports brought the war into people's living rooms in a very graphic way. Casualties were mounting daily. Feelings ran very high, particularly on college campuses.

Students at Harvard occupied the Administration Building and went on strike. Many young men at various schools refused to be inducted into the armed forces. Some burned their draft cards in an open show of protest. Other protesters actually fled the country rather than join in what they considered an unjust war.

Albert Gore, Sr. was a member of the Senate Foreign Relations Committee. He was an open and very vocal opponent of the war. Further, he thought that the American people were not being told the truth about the fighting. Newspaper reports were not the same as the information he got as a Foreign Relations Committee member. John Tyson commented:

> At that time his [Gore's] father was our real champion on the Foreign Relations Committee of the Senate. Al was sought after, so to speak, by a lot of radicals to join up with them and to give them information in terms of what his insights were, his political thoughts on the matter. But when things got too far, his sense—he's got good sense—when he sensed that things were getting out of proportion, out of balance, he shied away from those people.[5]

Every night, when going in to dinner, Gore

encountered a table full of anti-war petitions. Some were sponsored by very radical groups.

In January 1968 the Vietcong launched a series of savage and bloody attacks on South Vietnamese cities. This Tet Offensive—as it was called because it began at the time of the Vietnamese New Year or Tet—came as a surprise to the American public. The government and U.S. military commanders had reported that the war was going well, and that the Vietcong were weakening and would soon be defeated. How, then, was one to explain these ferocious battles? Senator Gore thought that the unexpected attacks were a good example of how the American people were being misled about the war.

Senator Gore faced a re-election campaign in 1970. In the past he had always been elected despite his liberal views in such areas as civil rights. Now, with his fervent opposition to the Vietnam War, he was fighting an uphill battle. Al Gore, Jr. had a very difficult decision to make. He was as opposed to the war as his father was. But after his graduation in the spring of 1969 he would surely be called to serve. Should he make some effort to avoid service?

Such an action would have several consequences. Surely it would further hurt his father's re-election chances. And it would mean that another young man from Carthage would have to go in Gore's place. Carthage is a small town. If Al Gore avoided military service not only would everyone in town know it, but Al Gore himself would know who had to go in his place.

Senator and Mrs. Gore were careful not to try to influence Al, Jr.'s decision. They felt it was his decision and his alone. Pauline Gore remarked, "We tried in every way that we could to keep that decision free of any influence that the decision would have on his father's race. And I think that maybe it did—it was free of it. I don't think he did it to help his father."[6]

According to Al Gore, Jr. the primary reason for enlisting was a simple one. As he explained it, "Everybody knew there was a kind of quota and if I didn't go, then one of my friends would have to go in my place."[7] So Gore decided to enlist in the U.S. Army.

Vietnam Experience

After basic training, Gore was assigned to Fort Rucker, Alabama. Before he had to report for duty, Al and Tipper were married on May 19, 1970. The wedding took place in Washington Cathedral, next door to St. Albans School. Canon Charles Martin, who had been Gore's headmaster, performed the ceremony. Music for the ceremony included both traditional selections and popular music of the day. One Beatles song was part of the ceremony.

Gore's close friend, Jim Landau, was best man. The ushers included two of Al Gore's cousins and Carthage pal Steve Armistead. Gore wore his Army dress uniform.

Tipper was attended by her cousin and Al's sister Nancy Gore Hunger as well as five bridesmaids. She wore a gown of lace and silk, and carried a bouquet of carnations and orchids. The ceremony was followed by a country club reception.

Life at Fort Rucker was anything but comfortable. The newlyweds found that a trailer was the only housing available to them. There were no restaurants in the town. For recreation Al Gore returned to his painting. He also managed to play pickup games of basketball. Based on tests taken at the time of his enlistment, he was assigned as a journalist and public affairs specialist in the post's information office.

Every weekend that he could get away, Al and Tipper went to Tennessee to campaign for Al Gore, Sr. Dressed in uniform, Gore made TV commercials with his father. They hoped that these commercials and other campaign appearances would help defuse the anti-war issue. As Albert Gore, Sr. saw it, "I have the same obligation as my son—to serve my country and the people of Tennessee."[1]

Gore's sister, Nancy Gore Hunger, ran her father's campaign. Her husband Frank Hunger campaigned in western Tennessee for his father-in-law. And, as usual, Pauline Gore was a tireless campaigner. So at any one point in time, four Gores were campaigning in Tennessee.

Senator Gore's Republican opponent William E. Brock ran a very negative TV campaign. He not only blasted Gore for his stance on the war, but he also accused Gore of being out of touch with Tennessee voters. Brock was successful in his attacks. He beat Albert Gore, Sr. by 46,344 votes.

In his concession speech, his eyes blazing, Gore said, "Someday, and someday soon, I know that the truth shall rise again in Tennessee.[2] Though Al Gore, Jr. discounted the idea, many people believed that Al Gore, Sr. was referring to his son.[3]

His father's defeat left Al Gore soured on politics. Commenting on Gore's reaction to the loss, John Seigenthaler, the publisher of *The Tennessean*, said:

> I think there was a great disillusionment because he looked upon his father as a great, dedicated, caring, sensitive, patriotic public servant, whose record had resulted in making the world safer, and whose name was on the interstates that run across the country. He had provided support for domestic programs that had made this Valley, this Tennessee Valley, a garden spot. And Al Gore felt that his father on the basis of all that, and on the basis of his intelligence and his service, simply deserved to be reelected.[4]

Bitterly disappointed and totally disillusioned, Al Gore shipped out for Vietnam on Christmas Day 1970.[5] When Gore arrived at his headquarters, based near the Saigon airfield, he was issued the standard M16 rifle and ammunition.

Al Gore was not able to accept the circumstances of the war, its brutality, and its atrocities.[6] He realized as he looked at the soldiers, or "grunts," as they were called, that this was a teenagers' war. The average age of soldiers in World War II had been twenty-six. The average age in the Vietnam War was nineteen. Gore himself was only twenty-two.

Morale among the troops was low. The war was primarily guerrilla warfare. Everyone had to constantly be on the alert. Bands of Vietcong soldiers, VC for short, would appear out of nowhere it seemed. They would attack and then melt back into the dense jungle. Booby traps such as land mines were also common. To make the situation worse, soldiers couldn't always tell who the enemy was.

When approached, villagers who sympathized with the Vietcong would suddenly toss a grenade and run. The grunts learned that the only safe thing to do was to shoot first and ask questions later. Al Gore was sickened by the way in which American soldiers were forced to fight. The Americans were not able to distinguish South Vietnamese, who were allies, from North Vietnamese, who were enemies.

Many Vietnamese villages were destroyed by "zippo brigades." Village huts were made of bamboo and thatched with dried vegetation. American troops would go through a village and burn down the huts. The soldiers set fire to them with cigarette lighters, and the Zippo was a favorite inexpensive cigarette lighter. Hence the term —"zippo brigade" was coined.

Gore enlisted in the army in 1969. He opposed the war in Vietnam, but he felt that he should serve anyway.

Gore noted the effects of Agent Orange, the chemical Americans sprayed from aircraft to defoliate the jungle. He wrote, "I went to Vietnam with the Army and vividly remember traveling through countryside that used to be jungle, but now looked like the surface of the moon. A herbicide called Agent Orange had cleared the jungle, and we were glad of it at the time, because it meant that the people who wanted to shoot at us had fewer places to hide."[7] In later years, when Gore learned the long-term effects of Agent Orange, he came to feel differently about it. Agent Orange is the suspected cause of birth defects in Vietnamese children and cancers in those people who were exposed to it. The chemical also left four million acres of cropland destroyed and barren for years to come.

Al Gore took his turn in the small fire bases located in the countryside. He had been in Vietnam for about three months when he sent home an account of how one of the fire bases was overrun. His story was published in *The Tennessean*. It ran in the March 21, 1971, issue of the paper. Fire Support Base Blue was a small compound near the Cambodian border. Of the 135 men stationed there, thirty-five were engineers. The rest of the soldiers were artillerymen who fired shells into Cambodia. Some artillerymen used eight-inch guns and others used "dusters"—40mm guns mounted on tracked vehicles.

On the night in question, February 22, there was no

moon. Most of the men watched a movie and then turned in early. Shortly after midnight a trip flare was set off on the outside strand of barbed wire. One of the dusters fired, and there was no more noise. Everyone not on duty went back to sleep. About two hours later they were awakened again, this time by a violent explosion. The American soldiers suspected that they were being shelled, and that an attack by the Vietcong would follow shortly. More explosions blew up the 40mm duster, one of the eight-inch guns, and various other targets in the compound. Suddenly everyone seemed to be shouting the dreaded words, "VC in the compound! VC in the compound!"

The first explosion had been a rocket-propelled grenade that had opened a hole in the wire mesh in front of the eight-inch gun. Twenty Vietcong soldiers had sneaked through the hole. No one saw them get in and they began blowing up the guns and other targets. The Vietcong were very well camouflaged, wearing nothing but shorts and small hats. Their bodies were completely covered with charcoal—even their eyelids.

In Gore's account, "Thompson, who was stationed at Fire Support Base Yeager when it was overrun in 1968, adds, 'You can't just sit there when you got VC in the compound. There's only one thing to do: that's find 'em and pin 'em down.'"[8] It fell to the engineers in the camp to search out the VC. Gore seems to have been

43

everywhere at once in reporting the ensuing action. And like a good reporter, he got people's names and their home towns and used the proper rank for each man mentioned.

There were problems in finding and capturing the Vietcong. It was impossible to see in the pitch-black, moonless night. The eight-inch gun that had been hit was burning with a live shell in it. Finally the men put it out using fire extinguishers. One of the VC was trying to escape by jumping over a double row of barbed wire. Max, the huge wolflike dog who was the camp mascot, leaped up and seized him by the throat. Max seemed to sense that one of the American soldiers was prepared to shoot the VC. When a flashlight was shone on dog and man, the dog dropped the man and moved out of the line of fire.

Over the next four hours all the Vietcong soldiers were captured. Through an interpreter the Americans learned that the Vietcong command had determined that the fire base had to be put out of commission. A few days before, the base's guns had hit a Vietcong hospital. The fire base engineers were lucky. Only three of the American men suffered minor injuries and there were no fatalities.

Gore ended his story, "That night at dinner there was a strong esprit and too many war stories. Then someone brought in an intelligence report that one of the fire bases in the area was going to be overrun on the night of February 22. 'Oh yeah? No kidding?'"[9]

Five months later Gore left behind the horrendous experiences in Vietnam and returned home. His tour of duty was over. But not until January 1973 would a peace agreement end direct U.S. military involvement in Vietnam.

Searching for a Career

Like many men who served in Vietnam both before and after him, Gore returned home deeply troubled by his experience.[1] He seemed at loose ends and unable to settle down to anything. Indeed, he gave the impression that he had no idea of just what it was he wanted to do.

Al and Tipper Gore went to live on the farm in Carthage. Here Gore began the process of healing after the horror of Vietnam. He had trouble sleeping, and often Tipper would wake in the night and find that Gore had gone out to walk around the farm. He spoke of "atonement for things he saw and did in Vietnam."[2] He put in a garden and seemed to find a kind of therapy in working the soil.[3]

Gore's father tried to interest him in local politics, but the disillusionment of his father's last campaign and defeat was still too fresh. Gore didn't want any part of politics. Albert, Sr. also wanted him to go to law school, but Gore resisted this idea as well.

Shortly before enlisting in the Army, in September 1969, Gore had set up a company to build houses. He formed this company with his father and family friend Walter Robinson. The men planned on laying out a housing development and then building the houses. Once out of the army and home in Carthage, Gore joined with Walter Robinson in the construction work.

Robinson was happy to have him. As he put it. "He [Gore] puts everything he has into every effort he makes, basically because he wants to do a good job with anything he's connected with."[4]

The first house built by Tanglewood Home Builders, Inc., as their company was called, was owned by Dalton Minchey. Minchey commented, "I just wish somebody else would build some more houses that good and that affordable in this day and time."[5]

In the fall of 1971 Al Gore enrolled in Vanderbilt University's Divinity School in Nashville, Tennessee. He took courses in the graduate school, mainly in philosophical subjects. Vietnam had left him with many troubling questions he wanted to try and find answers to. As he put it, "I was interested in a structured opportunity to explore the most important questions that I had in my life. . . . And it was one of the most valuable years I've ever spent. I found a lot better questions."[6]

Capitalizing on his experience as a journalist in the Army, Gore decided to ask John Seigenthaler, the editor of *The Tennessean*, for a job as a reporter. Frank Ritter, the deputy managing editor, interviewed Gore for the job.

Ritter used a technique in job interviews that was intended to reveal how the job candidate reacted to pressure. He would pose a hypothetical situation in which the reporter's editor ordered him to write a story that the reporter knew to be wrong. If the applicant said he would write the story, then Ritter would accuse him of violating his conscience. If the would-be reporter said he couldn't write something he knew was a lie, then Ritter would ask how he justified not following orders. Ritter used this scenario with Gore. Ritter recalled the interview as follows:

> Al had a sure sense of self. He refused to be intimidated and he didn't back up. When I asked, "What would you do if your editor ordered you to write a story you knew to be untrue?" he answered immediately. "I can't imagine that an editor would ever ask a reporter to do that. It would be unprofessional. But if it happened, I would resign before I violated my conscience." It was the best answer I've ever gotten to that question.[7]

At first Al Gore was assigned to the police beat, obituaries, local school news, and the like. Typical of

Gore's early assignments were the firing of a Metro firefighter for having long hair, burglaries, tavern brawls, and similar news.

On the occasion of the annual Nashville Christmas parade in 1971, which was being held for the forty-first time, the newsroom was desperately trying to come up with some fresh angle on the story. Gore had the idea of writing the account as seen through the eyes of Scrooge and Tiny Tim of Charles Dickens' *A Christmas Carol.* His idea proved to be an inspired one that resulted in a first rate piece of work.

Ritter commented on Al Gore's talents as a reporter:

> Al excelled in many ways. . . If he was late with his copy, frequently it was because he hated to stop digging and asking questions. He had those characteristics of curiosity and aggressiveness that you can't teach. You can teach writing—and Al soon learned to write very well—but you can't teach initiative and integrity. Fortunately, Al didn't need instructions in those areas.[8]

Gore's very first assignment on the paper was as a night reporter, and he commuted the 120-mile round trip from Carthage to Nashville. When this trip became too much, he rented a small apartment. Then he and Tipper decided to rent a small house in Nashville. Tipper Gore enrolled in a night school photography course in order to have something to do while Gore was working nights at the paper. She also decided to begin graduate study toward a master's degree in psychology.

Tipper Gore's photography class was taught by Jack Corn, the chief photographer on *The Tennessean* staff. He was impressed with her work and offered her a job. She worked several days a week in the photo lab and did picture assignments. Now both Gores worked for *The Tennessean.*

As many people presumed about Al Gore, some newspaper people thought that he was wealthy. Jerry Thompson was the reporter whom Gore was succeeding as police reporter. When Gore asked Thompson to go to the police station and introduce him, Thompson was pleased to do so.[9] He assumed that they would travel in Gore's Mercedes or Cadillac. When Gore stopped beside a very beat-up old Chevrolet and asked Jerry to hop in, Thompson was amazed.[10]

On their way to the station, a police officer gestured for them to pull over to the side of the road. The police officer told Gore that one of the car's headlights was not working. Gore jumped out of the car and kicked the defective light. It came on immediately, but shined off to the side rather than straight ahead. Gore gave it another kick, and the headlight swung around and pointed down the road. The police officer just shook his head in disbelief and waved Gore back inside his car. Thompson, who had had visions of impressing his police friends, now hoped no one would see them arrive.[11]

Even though he continued his courses at Divinity School, Al Gore worked hard at his newspaper job. Soon his work merited him promotion. Among other assignments he was asked to cover the Metro Council, Nashville's governing body. He became involved in two investigations, each one involving a payoff to a member of the Metro Council.

A businessperson came to Gore and told him that one of the Metro Council members was refusing to sponsor a certain bill that would make possible a building project. He alleged that unless the business person paid off the council member—to the tune of $1,000—the bill would not be introduced. Gore arranged for the businessperson to wear a recording device when he met with the council member. While the tape recorder got every word, Gore made sure that photographers from *The Tennessean* snapped good clear photos of the meeting. Gore was upset when the ensuing trial resulted in a mistrial and the council member was acquitted.[12]

Later, Gore uncovered an alleged payoff of a council member. This time the council member had allegedly been bribed with $2,500 to sponsor legislation that would affect a shopping center in his district. Though the council member was indicted, tried, and convicted, he did not serve any time in prison.

These experiences angered and frustrated Al Gore.[13] He decided that he needed to learn more about a legal system that would allow such situations to happen. Gore made the decision to go to law school.

Accordingly in 1974 Al Gore dropped out of Divinity School, took a leave of absence from the newspaper, and transferred to Vanderbilt's Law School. Al and Tipper's first child, named Karenna, had been born in August 1973. In that same year they bought a farm of eighty acres and a house outside of Carthage. They bought the property from Gore's parents, whose farm lay across the Caney Fork River.

Because they were both going to school and had jobs in Nashville, Al and Tipper Gore rented one half of a small duplex in Nashville. Gore had little more than one year remaining of law school. He attended classes in the morning and early afternoon. He worked nights again at *The Tennessean*, this time writing editorials.

Gore and Tipper decided that with law school almost completed it was time to buy a house. They found a brownstone house on nearly an acre of land in an old established neighborhood of Nashville. Both Gores were happy with their studies, work, and daughter. This was the situation when Al Gore answered a telephone call from John Seigenthaler. This phone call would set the course of Al Gore's career.

A Political Career Blooms

Al Gore was at home in Nashville in February 1976. He had finished his day at law school and was just about to leave for work when the phone rang. On the other end was his boss John Seigenthaler. He called to tell Gore that news had just come over the wire that Joseph L. Evins had announced his retirement as representative from the Fourth District. Joe Evins had served in Congress for thirty years.

Gore decided to enter the race. The first change he made was to start doing pushups to train for the rigors of the campaign. Other changes noticed by friends were that Al Gore stopped parting his hair in the middle and that he took to wearing suits. A dark blue suit and red tie became his campaign uniform.

Tipper Gore quit her job as a photographer on the

staff of *The Tennessean* to campaign full-time for her husband. Speaking of his first try at campaigning Gore later remembered:

> I walked out on the courthouse steps and made my first real speech announcing for Congress and I walked down the street shaking hands with the first person I saw asking for their vote and delivered the most awkward request for a vote you ever heard—it was tortured—but the next was easier and better and by the tenth or twelfth time I was in the groove.[1]

The Gores sold their Nashville home and moved to the Carthage farm.

Gore's sister Nancy worked hard on this first campaign. She was an extremely important person in Gore's life. Despite the ten-year difference in their ages, they were very close. Gore regarded her as both friend and adviser. She was a Vanderbilt University graduate who was captivated by the idea of service embodied in the Peace Corps. After her father took her to discuss the subject with President John F. Kennedy, she helped to get the Peace Corps started. After her Peace Corps service she worked abroad in Brussels for a time. She returned to Tennessee and went into the cattle business with her father. Nancy married Frank Hunger—a Greenville, Mississippi, lawyer.

Nancy was an enormous help to her brother because she was a seasoned political campaigner. She had managed several of her father's campaigns. Gore, his wife, mother, and sister campaigned hard all over Smith County and the rest of the Fourth District.

The primary was the really important election. The Fourth District always voted for a Democrat in the general election. Whoever won the Democratic primary was virtually assured of winning the general election in November. Al Gore supported positions that were populist, or people-centered. Though there were eight other candidates, Gore's main opponent was a Democratic state legislator named Stanley Rogers.

Rogers was hampered by the fact that the name "Gore" was one that had instant recognition in Tennessee and certainly in the Fourth District. Rogers tried to convince people that Al Gore was too young and inexperienced. When that argument didn't seem to work, he tried to paint Gore as wealthy. This attempt failed too. When the ballots were counted, Al Gore beat Rogers, his nearest opponent, by 3,559 votes. He won the general election with 96 percent of the vote!

As Al Gore began his service in the U.S. Congress, he began a pattern that he would continue to follow during his years in the House and Senate. He would fly home to Tennessee on Friday nights in order to hold town meetings. He would discuss issues with his constituents, and answer questions and address their concerns. Early Sunday mornings he would return to Washington in time to join his family for church.

Freshman Representative Al Gore, Jr. (center) chatted with then Attorney General Griffin Bell (left) after a swearing-in ceremony. His proud father (to Gore's left) joined him for the occasion.

During the time Al Gore served in Congress, he held more than 1,600 such town meetings.

Issues regarding health were some of those in which Gore took a keen interest. He sponsored a bill that required baby formula makers to include nutrients, such as chloride, in their product to promote healthy growth. This legislation was an outgrowth of his investigation that revealed that some baby formula lacked chloride. Babies fed only on this formula were underweight and listless, and didn't grow normally.

Gore also became interested in the question of organ transplants. He favored a bill that established a nationwide network to match organ donors with people needing transplants. This bill took into account how urgent the need for the organ was as well as other issues such as tissue typing. In addition the legislation outlawed the buying and selling of human organs. Gore told a news conference, "We must not allow technology to dehumanize people so that we erode the distinction between things and people. People should not be regarded as things to be bought and sold like parts of an automobile."[2]

Another of Al Gore's chief concerns was the subject of nuclear arms control. Initially Gore devoted little time or study to the subject. But the topic of nuclear weapons began to crop up more and more at his weekend town meetings. "I was kind of surprised by it," Gore said. "I gave the kind of stock answers you can get away with in this business, but then I asked a group of students how many of them thought there would be a major nuclear war in their lifetimes. About 85 percent raised their hands. I started hearing more and more about it. There was an enormous fear, enormous hopelessness."[3] From that time on Gore devoted at least eight hours each week to studying arms control and defense issues. After his election in 1980 he studied the problem and consulted with experts for thirteen months until he became an acknowledged expert himself.

Gore argued that the United States had no unified plan to follow in negotiating arms control issues with the Soviet Union, as the country was called then. In 1982 he presented his plan, which was a middle-of-the-road approach. The one question that made for instability, and therefore danger, was the question of the first strike. There was the danger that during a great political crisis, either the United States or the Soviet Union would be tempted to overreact and attack first.

Gore's plan called for a change in both U.S. and Soviet nuclear forces so as to reduce fear. He called for a new comprehensive arms agreement between the United States and the Soviet Union that would effect such a change. Writing in *The New Republic,* Gore said:

> If both sides were to carry out this change, neither would ever be in a position to make the arithmetic of a first strike work. Although either side could attack the other's intercontinental ballistic missiles

[ICBM], the attacker would have to use up his entire ICBM inventory to do the job . . . the side that struck first would find itself at a disadvantage even against the residual [remaining] forces of its enemy.[4]

The Soviet arms specialists were very interested in Gore's plan. It gained a great deal of support and was praised by many, including a senior columnist of *The New York Times.*

During his years in the House, Al Gore championed legislation on a subject that had long interested him—the environment. He held hearings on the subject of toxic waste dumps. He co-sponsored legislation that established a Superfund. The money in this fund was to be given to the states so that they could clean up sites where there were chemical spills and dangerous land dumps. The Superfund Law was just one of many bills that Gore would sponsor intended to help the environment.

In January 1983 Howard Baker, the Republican Majority Leader of the Senate, announced that he wouldn't seek re-election as senator from Tennessee. As soon as Gore heard the news, he planned to run for the seat. Gore was too well-known and popular to be challenged by anyone in the primary election, so he was able to concentrate on the general election campaign.

The Republicans fought among themselves during their primary campaign. The eventual winner was State

Al Gore announced his candidacy for the U.S. Senate from the steps of the Smith County Court House. He wanted to continue to follow in his father's footsteps and represent all of Tennessee.

Senator Victor H. Ashe. Ashe was a man disliked by both his Republican and Democratic colleagues. He liked to tease people in an unpleasant way and was often sarcastic.[5] A Republican primary candidate named Ed McAteer was angered by a national endorsement given to Ashe, and withdrew from the race.[6] Then in the November election McAteer ran as an Independent, siphoning votes away from Ashe.

Gore campaigned hard, as if he were an incumbent. On one hot and humid day in the summer, he was campaigning in a rural area. He happened on a softball game and began shaking hands with the spectators. Gore had spoken to everyone at the game and was about to leave when he spotted a pickup truck parked nearby. The truck's owner was stretched out underneath making some repairs. Gore asked him to come out from under the truck, but the man refused. Gore knelt down, asked for the man's vote, and stuck a campaign card in the cuff of the man's pants. Then, since he couldn't reach the truck owner's hand to shake it, he squeezed his ankle instead.

Nancy Hunger wasn't able to help in this campaign as she had in all previous ones. She was suffering from lung cancer and was in the hospital in Nashville. Gore stole every minute he could from campaign work in order to be with his sister. In July of that year, Nancy Hunger lost her battle with cancer. Al Gore was deeply affected by her death. In a TV interview, Pauline Gore observed:

> It was very difficult for him. We were all very close, although she was ten years older. He thought Nancy was indestructible. Al is a very compassionate person. He grew up very close to his grandparents and their loss was a very sad thing for him. It has contributed a dimension to him that will be reflected in the kind of person he is and the kind of feeling he has for the people he represents.[7]

Victor Ashe was no match for Al Gore, Jr. On election day 1984 Gore won with 61 percent of the votes. He even carried Ashe's stronghold of Knox County. It was on to the Senate for Al Gore, Jr.

Hard-Working Senator

Al Gore's decisive victory for the Senate in 1984 was even more impressive because there was a Republican landslide that year. However, his "easy" win did not affect his hard-working style. In the Senate, Al Gore continued to study the subjects and to champion the causes that had occupied him in the House. He asked to be assigned to two very important committees: Armed Services; and Commerce, Science, and Transportation.

As a member of the Armed Services Committee, Gore continued his study of questions relating to strategic arms and avoiding nuclear war. The Commerce, Science, and Transportation Committee was a natural choice for him because of his wide knowledge of technological matters. He urged that cable TV be more strictly regulated, arguing that the full potential of cable had barely been touched. He sponsored the National High Performance Computer Technology Act, legislation that would create a national super computer network. This network would link the country's schools and research laboratories with computers far more powerful than they could otherwise afford. He sponsored bills to develop new technologies and to spread word of them to industry.

On January 28, 1986, the space shuttle *Challenger* exploded after liftoff. The entire crew was killed, including civilian Christa McAuliffe, a New Hampshire schoolteacher. Construction and testing of the shuttle were the responsibility of the National Aeronautics and Space Administration (NASA). After the terrible *Challenger* disaster, it was Al Gore who held hearings that led to the realization that NASA had cut back on its quality monitoring.

Gore provided leadership in a variety of health care topics. He was responsible for a computerized network to match organ donors with people needing the transplants. He led the fight to strengthen the warning labels on cigarette packages and to place warning labels on alcoholic beverages.

However, the area of expertise in which Al Gore is best known is unarguably the environment. He was the principal sponsor of the resolution calling for Earth Day 1990 on April 22 of that year. Also he was chairman of the U.S. Senate delegation to the Earth Summit in June

1992, which was the largest meeting to date of heads of state considering environmental questions. He has initiated legislation in a wide range of environmental matters from cleaning up toxic waste sites to phasing out ozone-depleting chemicals. He has done everything possible to encourage recycling and to maintain strong markets for recycled products.

In money matters Gore favored higher income tax rates for households with taxable income over $110,000. He wanted to use the added revenue to give tax breaks to middle-class families with children. Gore opposed the argument that social security benefits should be given only to the needy.

In August 1990 Iraq's leader Saddam Hussein invaded Kuwait. President George Bush planned to send troops and to get the help of allies to drive Saddam's forces out of Kuwait. Al Gore criticized President Bush for not acknowledging Congress' power by asking for its approval. When the President finally did come to the Congress seeking approval of his plan, Gore wrestled with the issue, calling it "excruciating."[1] Finally deciding that Saddam Hussein's aggression should not be tolerated, Gore voted for the resolution that approved sending troops to the Persian Gulf.

The Republicans attacked those Democrats who had not supported the President. Al Gore quickly came to the defense of his colleagues saying, "The Republicans seem determined to load their big guns with cheap shots."[2]

In January and February 1991 the U.S.-directed coalition forces defeated Iraq after 6 weeks of bombing and 100 hours of ground attacks. The troops liberated Kuwait from occupying Iraqi forces, but they failed to topple Saddam Hussein from power.

It is unusual for a wife to testify before a Senate Committee of which her husband is a member. But in September 1985 Tipper Gore did just that, testifying in hearings before the Senate Commerce Committee. This unusual situation came about through the following events.

In December 1984 Mrs. Gore bought Prince's hit album *Purple Rain* for her eleven-year-old daughter Karenna. When they got home and played the album on their stereo, they were both horrified at a song called "Darling Nikki." As Mrs. Gore later recounted, "The vulgar lyrics embarrassed both of us. At first I was stunned—then I got mad!"[3] Mrs. Gore discussed the situation with her good friend Susan Baker, wife of then Secretary of Treasury James Baker. The Bakers had good reason to be concerned about what was being sold to young people—they have eight children. Mrs. Baker invited Mrs. Gore to join her in alerting parents about the obscenity and violence in rock music.

The women decided to establish a nonprofit group to be called Parents' Music Resource Center (PMRC).

The women sent invitations to parents, friends, community leaders, and representatives of the music industry to the first meeting of PMRC. They were surprised but delighted when 350 people attended.[4] No music representatives came to the meeting, but the president of the NAB (National Association of Broadcasters) asked his wife to attend.

The NAB suggested to record companies that they enclose written lyrics with the records they send to radio stations for disk jockeys to play on the air. The record companies resisted this idea, as did the radio stations. A representative for station KROQ-FM in Pasadena, California, commented, "The music is the beat; the lyrics come secondary."[5] The chairperson of Warner Brothers Records told the *Los Angeles Times*, "It smells of censorship. . . . Radio stations can make their own decisions about what they want to play."[6]

Members of PMRC launched a wide-ranging publicity campaign to bring the subject of obscenity in rock music to the attention of the public. They petitioned the recording industry to consider a rating system such as the film industry uses. They were told that such a system would be impossible. There are about 350 new films every year, but there are 2,500 new albums and 25,000 new songs each year. To rate them all would be out of the question.

At this point the recording companies fought back by saying that PMRC was trying to censor rock music artists and take away the musicians' constitutional right to free speech. PMRC replied that it was not trying to censor anyone and wanted more information, not less. The group wanted warning labels and/or printed lyrics visible on the outside packaging of records. It did not want to decide what needed a warning label. It felt that the record companies should make those decisions.

Groups opposed to the idea of warning labels quickly formed. Danny Goldberg, president of Gold Mountain Records, organized a group called the Musical Majority. The 100-member Citizens Against Music Censorship began a letter-writing campaign to elected officials and record companies.

There was also a storm of protest from the general public. *People Weekly*'s article on the labeling controversy drew a response of 2,035 letters—more than any other article in the history of the magazine! Of those commenting, 90 percent said they opposed what they considered censorship. When Ann Landers, the newspaper advice columnist, asked her readers to respond to a letter blaming rock and roll for teenaged behavior such as suicide and drug abuse, the response was overwhelming. Of the first 20,000 letters, 90 to 1 were pro-rock music.

At this point Republican Senator John Danforth of Missouri, chairperson of the Commerce Committee, decided to hold hearings on the subject. Both Al and Tipper Gore had misgivings about the hearings. Tipper

Gore said, "I thought the PMRC would be better off working with artists and the industry on their own terms, instead of dragging everybody before the TV cameras on Capitol Hill."[7] Tipper Gore testified for the PMRC, and of course, as a committee member, Al Gore heard her and others speak. The Senate hearing room was packed. As Mrs. Gore recalled, "A seat in the hearing room was the hottest ticket in town all year."[8] When Dee Snider of the group Twisted Sister testified, Senator Gore's questioning brought out the fact that even Snider's fan club had an obscene name.

As a result of the hearing, the PMRC struck a bargain with the recording industry. In return for a warning label stating "Explicit Lyrics—Parental Advisory" on offending records, the PMRC would consider the matter resolved. Mrs. Gore went on to write a book titled *Raising PG Kids in an X-rated Society,* which told the story of PMRC. In the book she offered parents further advice on many ways to protect their children from unwanted obscene material.

Her book was a success, and Tipper Gore began to travel the country on a promotional tour. Thus she was not as enthusiastic as she would have otherwise been when Al Gore decided to try for the Democratic presidential nomination in 1988.[9] She felt that they both should not be away from home at the same time.[10] A national campaign means hours on the road and very little time spent with family. Tipper agreed to support her husband's effort, however.

Six other candidates were in the running for the Democratic presidential nomination: former Colorado Senator Gary Hart, Senator Joseph Biden from Delaware, Representative Richard Gephardt from Missouri, Senator Paul Simon from Illinois, Massachusetts Governor Michael Dukakis, and—most influencing to Gore's chances—Reverend Jesse Jackson from Chicago. Jackson was the person who most threatened to draw away votes from Gore. As a very popular and well known African-American preacher, he would most likely capture votes of African Americans in the south—votes that otherwise would probably go to Al Gore.

Gore wanted to make the environmental crisis a main political issue, but he found the public uninterested in his cause. When he realized that he wasn't getting his message across, he turned to pollsters and political advisers for help. In changing his focus he was accused of tailoring his message, depending on where he was campaigning. Gore was further hampered by the stiff and wooden manner in which he delivered campaign speeches.

The purpose of the primary election is to allow the voters of each political party to indicate which candidate they prefer to run against the opposition candidate in the general election.

After eight years in the House of Representatives and four years in the Senate, Al Gore decided to try for the presidency. Surrounded by family, friends, and well-wishers, Gore announced that he was running.

The primary election process in Iowa is unusual. The voters do not go to the polls to elect the delegates for their preferred candidate. Instead all the delegates go to a meeting called a caucus. There, in one place at one time, they cast their votes for the candidate of their choice. Gore decided not to try for this early Iowa contest.

In New Hampshire, which prides itself on having the first primary election, he made only a modest effort. He was accompanied there by his friend and fellow Tennessean, country singer Johnny Cash. Gore's strategy was to concentrate on what had come to be called Super Tuesday, a single Tuesday in March during which fourteen southern states hold their primaries. As Gore said, "If you're going duck hunting, you go where the ducks are. Forty percent of all the delegates to the National Democratic Convention in July are in Super Tuesday states and that's where I'm going hunting."[11] His main rival was, of course, Jesse Jackson. When the votes were counted, Gore had won five states outright. Though he didn't overwhelm his opposition, he managed to stay in the race.

The crucial test would be New York State. Though the primary involved the entire state, New York City—with its large number of Democrats—was the most important prize. In New York City, Gore was joined in his campaign by the city's current mayor Edward I. Koch. Koch's endorsement proved to be a disaster. Koch was engaged in open warfare with Jesse

Jackson. There had also been several recent racial incidents in the city. One of these involved a conflict between African Americans and the Jewish community. Mayor Koch, a Jew, used campaign appearances with Gore to lambaste Jesse Jackson.

Frequently Gore had a hard time getting a word in when he appeared with Koch. To make matters worse, Koch was at this point rather unpopular in the city. His behavior angered people and some of this anger transferred to Al Gore. Even though he was one of only three Democrats still in the primary, Gore won only 10 percent of the New York State vote. Two days later he suspended his campaign.

A loyal Democrat, Al Gore campaigned vigorously for the eventual nominee Governor Michael Dukakis. His efforts were to no avail, however. George Bush went on to win the presidency in November 1988. Al Gore would have to wait for four years before a chance would come for him to try again. Meanwhile there was still work to be done as a U.S. senator.

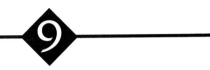

The Environmental Cause

It was not until the 1960s that the public began to get really upset about the environment. As William Ruckelshaus, the first administrator of the Environmental Protection Agency (EPA) said:

> Public support only began to explode in the late 1960s. It led to creation of the EPA, which never would have been established had it not been for public opinion. That I am absolutely certain of. Public opinion remains *absolutely essential* for anything to be done on behalf of the environment.[1]

Al Gore first became aware of the necessity for preserving the environment on the farm in Carthage. His father taught him to stop a gully by filling it up. Otherwise the gully would become a ditch and precious topsoil would be washed away. In 1962 a book by

Rachel Carson, *Silent Spring*, warned about the dangers of DDT and other pesticides. This book made a deep impression on Al's mother. She stressed the lessons of *Silent Spring* to Al and his sister Nancy. So from a very early age Al Gore was concerned about the environment.

In 1978 Representative Al Gore had received a letter from a family in Toone, Tennessee. They had been experiencing sickness that they thought was caused by a toxic waste dump. A Memphis company had bought a neighboring farm and was using ditches dug on the farm as a dump site for pesticide waste. Millions of gallons of hazardous waste leaked into the well water of area farms. Gore decided to hold congressional hearings on the subject of toxic waste. He focused on Toone and also on one other site at Niagara Falls, New York. That second site became celebrated as the most terrible example of the hazards of toxic waste dumping. It was called Love Canal.

Love Canal was named after its creator William Love. Love began the canal to carry water to generate electricity. His scheme fell through and the canal was left unfinished. Years later the Hooker Chemical and Plastics Corporation used the site as a dump for its toxic waste. The land was then needed for residential development, and the canal was filled in. The city of Niagara Falls built a new elementary school right in the middle of what proved to be a fearsome toxic waste dump. Forty-two million pounds of chemical wastes, including many that were proven to cause cancer, had been dumped in the old canal. In time, these wastes leaked into the water supply with terrible consequences. Women suffered miscarriages and stillbirths, babies were born with defects, and both children and adults had serious physical illnesses. The entire area of Love Canal had to be evacuated, and its population relocated, costing the federal and state government $28 million.

The legislative outcome of Gore's congressional hearings was the Superfund Law. In 1980 Gore and others managed to push through this measure, which provided a fund of $1.6 billion to clean up toxic waste sites.

As a member of the U.S. House Energy and Commerce Oversight Subcommittee, Al Gore looked into the problem of illegal hazardous waste dumping. He found that haulers were taking waste and dumping it anywhere they could. Some haulers just turned a faucet and let liquid hazardous waste drain out of their tankers as they drove around the country. Organized crime got involved in illegal dumping of waste on roadsides or in rivers, usually in the dead of night. Partly as a result of Gore's exposure of these practices, the Justice Department began cracking down and bringing criminal charges against illegal dumpers.

Gore realized that it is necessary to protect the American people from imported products that do not measure up to U.S. standards. In 1985 he was the author

Leaking barrels like these create toxic waste dumps. Gore sponsored legislation, known as the Superfund Law, meant to pay for clean-up of sites like this.

and sponsor of an amendment to prohibit the import of tobacco that had been grown with pesticides that are prohibited in the United States as unsafe.

Though Gore realized that recycling is mostly a local matter, he was the author of legislation to encourage recycling. As more and more communities joined in recycling efforts, markets for recycled materials began to dry up. Gore was the author of legislation that strengthened the market for recycled goods.

In a totally new effort to promote cooperation between military and civilian scientists and researchers, Gore sponsored the Environmental Research Program. This program makes the research of both groups available to the other. In this way each group is helped in its work to understand the global environment.

Al Gore traveled many thousands of miles on fact-finding trips to gather firsthand information about environmental matters. In 1988 Gore traveled to the South Pole to witness the beneficial effects of the Clean Air Act. A scientist had dug a core sample which showed annual layers of ice from the glacier on which he and Gore were standing. The scientist pointed out the layer of twenty years before when Congress passed the Clean Air Act. Even a small amount of reduction in U.S. emissions affected the pollution to be found in polar ice.

Scientists at the South Pole also measure the effect of global warming. Several times a day scientists monitor the air. Gore watched as one scientist drew the result of that day's measurements. The line showing the warming trend went upward on the graph. The change in global atmosphere caused by high levels of carbon dioxide is increasing rapidly.

In 1989 Gore visited the South American nation of Brazil to observe the threatened Amazon rain forest. Every year a portion of the rain forest is burned to turn the land into pasture for beef cattle. Every minute of every day in the year, an area equivalent to 200 football fields of forest is destroyed. These forests were home to many species of animals and plants. In describing his visit, Gore remarked that the biologist Tom Lovejoy told him that ". . . there are more different species of birds in each square mile of the Amazon than exist in all of North America—"which means we are silencing thousands of songs we have never heard."[2] In Haiti, where timber is cut to use for fuel, less than 5 percent remains of the lush forests that once covered the country.

The result of rain forest destruction is not only loss of species, however. There is another consequence just as important. Soil erosion is greatly increased when there are no trees to hold the soil in place. On the island country of Haiti, one quarter of its exposed soil is rapidly eroding.

Gore saw the results of a scheme in Central Asia to

This aerial view of the island of Hispanola shows the effect of cutting down the rain forest. The contrast between Haiti on the left, where most trees have been destroyed, and the Dominican Republic on the right, where they have not, is stark.

divert the water flowing into the Aral Sea in order to grow cotton. He described his 1990 trip to what was once the fourth-largest inland sea in the world:

> I was standing in the sun on the hot steel deck of a fishing ship capable of processing a fifty-ton catch on a good day. But it wasn't a good day. We were anchored in what used to be the most productive fishing site in all of central Asia, but as I looked out over the bow, the prospects of a good catch looked bleak. Where there should have been gentle blue-green waves lapping against the side of the ship, there was nothing but hot dry sand—as far as I could see in all directions.[3]

The shoreline had retreated twenty-four miles and the fishing fleet was docked for good.

In 1991 Gore visited the North Pole. This was the site of an exchange of information between ice scientists and the U.S. Navy. The data from submarine sonar tracks, which had been top secret, was exchanged as a result of his Environmental Research Program. The ice scientists use the data to help them learn what is happening to the north polar cap. They find that, as at the South Pole, carbon dioxide levels are rapidly rising and causing warming in the polar region.

While many species of animals are lost because of the destruction of the rain forests that are their habitat, there are animal species in other habitats that are also endangered. Gore went to East Africa where, as he put it, "I encountered the grotesquely horrible image of a dead elephant, its head mutilated by poachers who had dug out its valuable tusks with chain saws."[4]

He also visited the Caribbean and noted the bleached condition of the coral reefs. Warmer ocean temperatures kill the organisms that live in the reef and give the reef its color. Scientists have noted growth in the number of these bleaching occurrences. When bleaching is occasional and temporary, the coral recovers. Now, all too often, reefs fail to revive.

Through countless hours of hearings and thousands of miles of travel, Al Gore became the acknowledged expert on the environment in Congress. He would share what he had learned and what he thought we should do with that knowledge.

Earth in the Balance

On April 3, 1989, Senator and Mrs. Al Gore took their son Albert to the season opener of the Baltimore Orioles baseball team. The game was an exciting one as the Orioles beat the American League East Champions, the Boston Red Sox, 5–4, in a game that ran to eleven innings. The Gores were leaving Memorial Stadium when, as Senator Gore later recounted, "I . . . saw my son, Albert, then six years old, get hit by a car, fly thirty feet through the air, and scrape along the pavement another twenty feet until he came to rest in a gutter."[1] Albert Gore, III, hovered between life and death for days and for the next month Gore and his wife stayed at the hospital at Albert's side. Watching his son almost die was to change Al Gore's life and future in very drastic ways. Gore explained the change this way:

> For me something changed in a fundamental way. I don't think my son's brush with death was solely responsible, although that was the catalyst. But I had also just lost a presidential campaign; moreover, I had just turned forty years old. I was, in a sense, vulnerable to the change that sought me out in the middle of my life and gave me a new sense of urgency about those things I value the most.[2]

The outpouring of sympathy from people in all walks of life and their sharing of their own experiences made Al Gore newly self-aware. He realized that people he knew such as elevator operators and secretaries carried burdens and tragedies and that he had never even noticed them.[3] As Gore later said, "I'm almost embarrassed to think about the degree to which I was unaware of that dimension in the way we relate to one another.[4]

Al Gore began a search for the meaning of relationships: within himself, with his family, and between people and their environment. Above all, Gore reexamined his relationship to the environment in large and small ways. He borrowed the use of a nurse's station near Albert's hospital room and began writing the book that would become *Earth in the Balance: Ecology and the Human Spirit.*

Albert's recovery, which was eventually complete,

was to be slow and long. He had sustained massive injuries both internally and externally. Operations and skin grafts were part of the lengthy process of healing. The terrible accident and its aftermath were a traumatic time. The entire Gore family went into therapy. Speaking of the counseling they received, Tipper Gore said, "It was extremely helpful to us. . . . If there's a problem or traumatic event in your life, don't be afraid to seek counseling.[5]

During Albert's long convalescence, Gore worked on his exhaustive study of the environment. He wrote mostly at night either at his parents' Washington, D.C., apartment or at home. In the introduction to the book he describes Albert's accident. Talking to Michael Kelly of *The New York Times* about writing that introduction, Gore said:

> The words finally broke through and came through my fingers out of the keys. . . . I could not control the emotion. . . . I was just sobbing as I was putting it, as the words were finally falling out of me. And it was one of the most intense and painful and moving experiences I ever had in finally allowing myself to put that into words.[6]

In *Earth in the Balance* Gore examines how "the various parts of nature interact in patterns that tend toward balance and persist over time."[7] He stresses that people are a part of nature just as much as natural forces like the tides and the wind. He also stresses that we are

89

the force that is a threat to our world and is pushing it out of balance. He says:

> Indeed, until our lifetime, it was always safe to assume that nothing we did or could do would have any lasting effect on the global environment. But it is precisely that assumption which must now be discarded so that we can think strategically about our new relationship to the environment.[8]

The word *strategically* in that last sentence is important. Gore notes that in order to classify the threats to our planet it is useful to use the military's system of looking at warfare. A conflict is either local, as in a skirmish or brief fight between small groups; regional, as in a battle; or a full-blown strategic war. Air pollution, water pollution, and illegal waste dumping are local in nature. A sulpherous smokestack or chemical waste dumped in a stream are local threats. Acid rain, on the other hand, is regional, covering a wide area. The sort of threat that is "strategic" is one such as global warming. This threat affects the entire climate of the globe.

Two factors, Gore tells us, have changed the relationship of people and Earth. First we have experienced an explosion of population. He notes that from the appearance of human beings on earth 200,000 years ago until 1945 it took more than ten thousand generations to reach a world population of two billion. From 1945 to 1992, in just two generations, the population of the world rose to 5.5 billion.

Second, we have seen a scientific and technological explosion which has transformed the ways in which we can exploit the earth. The automobile is a blessing that makes us mobile. But burning gasoline to make the car run releases carbon monoxide into the air, causing air pollution. Giant tankers can transport huge amounts of oil, a vital energy source. But oil spills such as the 1989 spill from the *Exxon Valdez* in Prince William Sound, Alaska, pollute entire areas and kill wildlife.

Gore titled the first section of his book "Balance at Risk." In this section he discusses various issues: the effects of global warming; the effects of climate on civilization; air pollution; the importance of water, seeds, and plants; the earth's surface; and waste of all kinds.

In the second section of the book, "The Search for Balance," Gore tries to explain how and why we created the threats that he says have become so apparent. He cites our political systems, run by politicians who don't want to spend the money it would take to redress the environmental balance. He observes that our economic system doesn't take into account environmental costs.

In the book's final section, "Striking the Balance," Gore offers what he calls a Global Marshall Plan. Gore insists that since the problem of the environment is a global one, only a global approach has any hope of success. A similar global problem was the devastation of Europe caused by World War II. In 1947 in a postwar commencement address at Harvard University, Secretary of State General George C. Marshall offered a plan to rebuild Europe. The Marshall Plan allowed Europe to use American financial aid in ways agreed upon by Europeans.

The plan was a large cooperative effort. Gore feels that the Marshall Plan could serve as a model for a new approach to the environment. He stresses that one of the important aspects of the plan was that it was regional. Every action had to be coordinated with all of the countries in a region. In a similar fashion it is vital that actions affecting the environment be global in scope.

Gore offers the following five strategic goals for the Global Marshall Plan: 1) World population must be stabilized. 2) We must create and develop new technologies to deal with environmental problems. 3) We must start to measure the economic impact of our decisions about the economy. 4) We must enter into new international agreements about the environment. 5) We must form a cooperative plan to educate the world about the environment.

As a general integrating goal, Gore notes that we must establish social and political conditions that will sustain stable societies. Contributory factors to social stability are justice, respect for human rights, good nutrition, health care, shelter, literacy, and political freedom—all necessary for all people.

Gore discusses his strategic goals in some detail. In terms of his first goal, Gore sees three conditions as necessary in order to halt the growth of world population. First, literacy and education must be made a top priority. This is true especially for women. When well educated, women are able to make informed decisions about the number of children they want to have. Second, because parents need to know that their children have a good chance of growing up, infant mortality must be lowered and children's good health insured. Third, family planning programs must be made available.

As an example of how population growth can be stabilized, Gore recounts the experience of provincial leaders in the Kerala province in southwestern India. The leaders there educated people, especially women. They lowered infant mortality; parents no longer felt they had to have many children in order to insure there would be someone to care for them in old age. Finally they provided family planning information. The population growth is now zero. Gore notes, "The consequences [of these actions] are little short of remarkable: in an area of the world characterized by uncontrollable population growth, Kerala's rate more nearly resembles Sweden than nearby Bombay."[9]

To attain his second strategical goal, Gore proposes a number of ways in which new technologies can be developed and old or discredited technologies phased out. Among other proposals, he would use taxes as rewards or punishments, depending on whether the environment is helped or harmed.

But new technologies must not only be created and developed, they must also be shared. The countries of the earth are at different stages of development. And some countries must be donators of technology while others must be receivers. In addition we must make a careful study of the environmental impact of any new technology before deciding that it is beneficial. Gore's discussion of agriculture provides a good example of new technology that may be harmful. In his discussion, Gore notes that by using technological advances, the third world has made great strides in increasing food production. However, these advances have not been without harm to the environment. Third-world farmers relied on heavy use of such technology as chemical fertilizers and pesticides, which caused pollution. Also poor irrigation schemes wasted water and poor farming methods led to soil erosion. Our new knowledge in areas such as irrigation technology, soil erosion management, development of plants that are naturally resistant to pests and disease, and imaginative crop rotation—all these techniques—must be shared.

Gore suggests a number of important changes that must be made as we evaluate the future consequences of our decisions—his third strategic goal. He calls for new accounting methods to be used. At present, countries assume that everything is without limits and is free. We must consider the depletion of natural resources in calculating a nation's worth. If a country clear-cuts its rain forest to sell the timber, that sale adds to the nation's wealth. But that country must be made to take into account that it can't sell that same rain forest the next year.

Further, we must take into account what impact our actions will have on the environment of future generations. Tribal councils of the Iroquois nation, Gore tells us, consider as best they can the effect of their decisions seven generations hence, which is about 150 years. Gore suggests that although the impact of some decisions is unknowable, we could learn much from the Iroquois' approach.

We must think of imaginative ways of using finance to promote preservation of the environment. Brazil, for example, is engaged in a "debt-for-nature" swap. In such a trade, the debt of developing nations that is owed to industrialized nations is forgiven. In return, the developing nation agrees to an enforceable protection of the environment.

Gore's fourth goal is the creation of new treaties and agreements among nations. He says that all such accords must be global in scope. In order for any such agreement to be successfully carried out, there must be a sharing of costs between the industrial nations and poor nations.

There must also be regular review of these treaties and agreements. And amendments must be made to these agreements as necessary. Gore says that the United States, as the only remaining superpower, must assume a leadership role.

Gore's fifth strategic goal involves a fundamental change in how we collect information about the environment. He suggests using the world's school-children in gathering information about the environment. For example, more accurate information about Earth's climate could be gained from widespread measurements of such factors as wind speed, humidity, and barometric pressure. These measurements could be made by schoolchildren all over the globe, while educating them about the environment's importance.

We must form a new global consensus about the environment and people must be convinced that the global environment is their "backyard." Gore notes that NIMBY ("not in my backyard") is a powerful force. If people truly believe that the world is their backyard, they will not be willing to see it polluted.

In the book's concluding chapter, Gore discusses the importance of change. He believes that while the Cold War—the long struggle against communism that lasted from 1945 until 1989—was being waged, we all had some doubts about the future of the planet. Now, with the Cold War a threat of the past, we should be even more optimistic. Gore believes we must have faith in the future. As he writes at the end of the book:

> For civilization as a whole, the faith that is so essential to restore the balance now missing in our relationship to the earth is the faith that we do have a future. We can believe in that future and work to achieve and preserve it, or we can whirl blindly on, behaving as if one day there will be no children to inherit our legacy. The choice is ours; the earth is in the balance.[10]

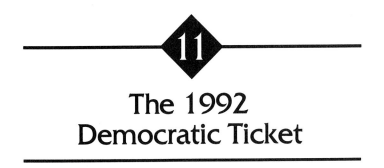

The 1992
Democratic Ticket

As the 1992 presidential election approached, Al Gore had an important decision to make. "You run with all your heart and soul and you're in there and you're going to rip the lungs out of anybody else in the race, and do it right."[1] Al Gore was describing to reporters his view of what a national presidential primary campaign would be like. The question was whether or not Al Gore was willing to make such an effort one more time in 1992. He knew that if he ran he would have to win the nomination. Someone running for the first time might survive a showing of second or even a strong third. But for Gore, after his loss in 1988, losing would perhaps mean the end of his presidential hopes.

There was a deeper and much more important consideration for Al Gore as he pondered the question of running. An article in *The Economist* pointed out, "Every week for the next year he would have had to ask 20 rich people for money, shake the hands of 200 less rich people, make the same speech 20 times, read a dozen articles about his private life and watch his every gesture for a single careless mistake."[2] The phrase about his private life was the one that mattered most. Albert III, was whole and well again after his dreadful accident. But the terrible experience and his son's long recuperation had fundamentally changed Al Gore. He said:

> It was during that experience of healing that I made the decision not to run for president in the 1992 cycle. And I wanted very much to run for president, but weighing that important goal against the duties that I had and enjoyed as a father and husband, in a family that was still in the midst of this healing process, the choice, though difficult, was in the end a rather obvious choice, and though I struggled with it, once I made it, I knew it was the right decision. And then for a year, I really enjoyed not running for president, and our family enjoyed not being involved in that race.[3]

The Democratic primary campaign was in full swing, minus Al Gore. President George Bush was certain to be nominated by the Republicans for a second term. A still unknown factor in the campaign was H. Ross Perot. This feisty billionaire businessman from Texas had stumbled into the campaign, more or less by accident—or so it seemed.

In a February appearance on the cable television talk show *Larry King Live,* the host had challenged Perot to run for President. Perot, off the top of his head it seemed, agreed that if his supporters would get his name on the ballot in all fifty states, he would declare himself an independent candidate. His main interest in running was his disenchantment with each of the two major parties. As Perot gained in popularity and increased in voting power, negative publicity about him began to surface. Reports emerged that Perot had ordered investigations—including one of George Bush—by private detectives.[4]

Meanwhile five Democrats were vying for the nomination. Former Massachusetts Senator Paul Tsongas had been the first to enter the race. He felt that the U.S. economy was in big trouble. Governor Bill Clinton of Arkansas felt the same way. In fact he had a sign tacked up in his campaign headquarters that read, "It's the economy, stupid!" Senator Tom Harkin from Iowa was an avowedly old-fashioned liberal. He supported large-scale public works projects. Nebraskan Senator Bob Kerrey counted on support because he was a war hero. Former California Governor Jerry Brown believed that America was run by special interests. After various primaries were held, Governor Bill Clinton emerged as the front runner. One by one the Democratic candidates pulled out of the race until only Bill Clinton and Jerry Brown remained. The all-important New York State primary in September would decide who the winning candidate would be. Clinton emerged the victor.

A few days after his victory in the New York primary, Bill Clinton talked to key advisors about the possibilities for a running mate. Clinton told them what criterions were important. The person chosen should share the same values that Clinton had, should have complementary strengths, and should be ready to serve as President from day one if the need arose.

A presidential candidate usually chooses a running mate from a different part of the country to widen the ticket's appeal. But Clinton stressed that his running mate's home state didn't matter. He felt that TV had made geography irrelevant.

Two weeks later on April 23, in a Florida hotel room, Clinton met with his search team. They considered a list of forty names. Suggestions were sought from many people in and outside of government. Al Gore was serving at the Rio de Janeiro Environmental Conference when California attorney Warren Christopher, head of the search team, phoned to ask for Gore's suggestions.

Al Gore named several people he thought would serve with distinction. At the end of the conversation, Christopher asked—almost casually—if Gore himself would be interested in the job. Gore asked for time to think it over. He soon decided that he was definitely interested. The vice presidential campaign would last only three months and wouldn't disrupt his family in the way a presidential bid would have.

At last a final short list was compiled. It included the names of several members of Congress—one of them Al Gore. Clinton met with each of the people being considered. He met with Gore in a long meeting held in the Capital Hilton Hotel on June 30.

On Wednesday night, July 8, 1992, Clinton held a meeting in the east conference room of the executive mansion in Little Rock, Arkansas. There, with key members of his search committee and his wife Hillary Rodham Clinton, he led the discussion about a choice for Vice President. Factors weighing heavily in favor of Al Gore were, first, his ability to step in and serve as President from day one. He had been tested before in a national campaign and he and Clinton thought alike on most important issues. Gore was also physically strong, which is important considering the energy needed to wage a vigorous campaign.

Furthermore, Gore had strengths Bill Clinton did not. He had a strong environmental record and he had served in Vietnam. There was one other reinforcing factor—two southerners on the ticket might just be enough to capture some southern states that the Republicans had always won previously. The meeting lasted for several hours. It ended when Bill Clinton asked what Al Gore's phone number was.

The entire Gore family immediately went to Little Rock. There Bill Clinton presented his choice of a running mate to reporters and the nation. In doing so he said:

> The running mate I have chosen is a leader of great strength, integrity, and stature; a father who, like me, loves his children and shares my hunger to turn this economy around, to change our country, and to do it so that we don't raise the first generation of children to do worse than their parents. The man standing beside me today has what it takes to lead this nation from the day we take office—Senator Al Gore of Tennessee.[5]

When Clinton finished his remarks, it was Gore's turn to speak. He began:

> I can tell you truthfully, I didn't seek this. And up until very recently when I began to get an inkling that I would get the call that came late last night, I didn't expect it. But I'm here for one simple reason: I love my country. And I believe in my heart that this ticket gives our country the best chance for the change we so desperately need—to move forward again.[6]

In these remarks Clinton and Gore sounded the two main themes of the campaign: that the economy was in big trouble and that the country was hungry for change.

From Little Rock, both families went to Carthage. There on the steps of the Smith County courthouse—where Gore had announced every previous bid for

After choosing Al Gore as his running mate, Bill Clinton spoke to the crowd at Carthage. The Gores and the Clintons made Gore's Tennessee home the first stop after leaving Little Rock.

office—both Gore and Clinton spoke to the crowd. Both men extolled the values and love of community that characterize small-town America. They promised to bring these fundamental beliefs back to the American people.

Reaction to the choice of Al Gore was almost uniformly favorable. The strength he would bring in the south was readily apparent. Former opponents of Bill Clinton had good things to say about his selection of Al Gore. The only prominent Democrat who was a detractor was Jesse Jackson who said, "I have deep concerns about the ticket. It takes two wings to fly and here you have two of the same wing."[7]

Having held what one could consider their first campaign rally in Carthage, the Democratic ticket prepared for the convention, now just days away.

Vice President Gore

As Al Gore finished his acceptance speech to thunderous applause at the Democratic convention, his family joined him on the podium. The band struck up singer Paul Simon's song "You Can Call Me Al." Gore embraced Tipper and began to dance with her around the podium. Then it was time for the climax of the evening—Bill Clinton's acceptance speech. Clinton spoke at some length before he said, "In the name of those who do the work, pay the taxes, and play by the rules—in the name of the hard-working Americans who make up our forgotten middle class—I proudly accept your nomination."[1] The speech making over, the evening ended in applause, cheers, and music. Everyone, it seemed, was dancing and hugging. The convention had been glorious.

Meanwhile, just the day before, something very important had happened. Ross Perot, who had never formally declared his candidacy, announced that he was withdrawing. His reason was that the Democratic party had revitalized itself. There was no way he could win in November in a three-way race. Privately, officials of Perot's Texas campaign said that the many unfavorable news stories had shaken Perot. Whatever the reason for Perot's action, it was a two-person race again.

As soon as the convention was over, the Clintons and Gores set off on a six-day, eight-state bus tour to campaign in small-town America. They capitalized on the surge in the public opinion polls the convention had created. The tour, which culminated in a rally in St. Louis, was a huge success. The dual campaigning allowed the candidates and their wives to get to know each other better. Clinton and Gore liked each other immediately, and Hillary Clinton and Tipper soon became fast friends.[2] The Gores had been scheduled to leave the tour after a few days, but it was such a success that they stayed for the whole trip.

President Bush was not yet actively campaigning, and the Republicans were way down in the polls. The situation got so bad that Bush called his friend James A. Baker, III, who had managed his 1988 campaign. He asked Baker to leave his job as secretary of state and take charge of the re-election effort. Al Gore called Baker's reassignment "a sign of extraordinary panic."[3]

In August the Republicans met in Houston. Their convention was marked by dissension, with basic differences erupting over party policy. Almost no platform plank was adopted without a fight. In his acceptance speech, President Bush vowed to stage the kind of come-from-behind win that President Harry Truman had managed in 1948. At last Bush was in what he called his campaign mode.

The question of presidential and vice presidential debates had been a problem. The number, format, and time and place of the debates had to be settled. Finally four debates, three presidential and one vice presidential, were agreed to by both parties. The vice presidential debate, in which Gore would participate, would be held on October 13 in Atlanta, Georgia.

Meanwhile Ross Perot reentered the race on October 1. It was a three-person race again. Perot had selected retired Admiral James Stockdale, who had spent years in a North Vietnamese prison camp, as his vice presidential running mate. So it was Stockdale, Gore, and Vice President Dan Quayle who met to debate at Georgia Tech in Atlanta on the night of October 13, 1992.

The format was one that allowed Gore and Quayle to directly oppose each other. Only one moderator asked questions, and he allowed the two major candidates to fling accusations at each other. Admiral Stockdale, who at one point had found that his hearing aid was turned off, stayed pretty much on the sidelines.

Washington Bureau Chief R. W. Apple reported on the debate in *The New York Times* the next morning. Calling Quayle's words crisp, Apple wrote that ". . . he [Quayle] gave a far better focused summary of the Republican case than his boss President Bush managed in his first encounter with Bill Clinton. . . ."[4] Apple gave full marks to Gore for his performance, writing "He [Gore] seemed more Presidential than Mr. Quayle, who often resorted to flippant asides. . . ."[5] When public opinion polls were taken of who did the best job, 50 percent of the respondents said Gore, 32 percent said Quayle, and 7 percent said Stockdale.

Late in October, President Bush was running well behind Clinton. It seemed that the Democratic strategy was paying off—two southerners were making a difference in the southern states. Clinton and Gore decided to make one last bus tour through the south.

Meanwhile the President began to sound frantic. He took to calling Al Gore "Ozone Man." In a Michigan campaign speech, Bush said, "My dog Millie knows more about foreign policy than these two bozos."[6]

As the campaign wound down in its final days, Al Gore consciously changed the tone of his speeches. He began to notice signs being held up by the crowd and to respond to hecklers. He noted a sign that said "I love Mr. Ozone."

"He seems to like *Zs*,"[7] Gore said, referring to Bush having called him "Ozone Man," and him and Clinton "bozos." Recalling the rest of Bush's accusation about foreign policy, Gore said, "Maybe it was Millie that told him to roll over and play dead on domestic policy."[8]

Finally the exhausting campaign was over. Now the people would speak via the ballot box. The Gores voted, as usual, at the Fork River Middle School in Carthage. Then the Gore family went to Little Rock to await the election returns. At 12:30 A.M. EST on November 4, Bill Clinton proclaimed victory at the Old State House in Little Rock. The final count gave Clinton-Gore, 43 percent; Bush-Quayle, 38 percent; and Perot-Stockdale, 19 percent.

With the election over many people wondered how important Gore's role would be in the new administration.[9] Any doubt about his influence was laid to rest by the boss himself. Speaking just before the inauguration, Clinton said, "He's [Gore's] been an integral part of picking a sub-Cabinet, an integral part of picking a White House staff. He's an integral part of policymaking. We have an astonishingly good relationship, I think, and it's really a full thing."[10]

Inaugural week in January 1993 arrived, and it began with a symbolic ride. Clinton wanted to demonstrate how much emphasis he placed on common people. How better to do that than by a symbolic bus ride to Washington, D.C., from Thomas Jefferson's home, Monticello, near Charlottesville, Virginia. Jefferson, one of Clinton's heroes, had stressed the

After voting at Fork River School, Al and Tipper Gore visited with
students. Gore never loses an opportunity to find out what people,
even the youngest of them, are thinking.

common person. Such a ride would allow a dramatic entrance to the Capitol Mall where the hoopla had already begun. A huge musical celebration with outstanding music stars would begin with the arrival of the Clintons and Gores. The two couples came down the steps of the Lincoln Memorial on cue, as trumpets blared a salute and twenty-one air force jets screamed overhead flying in tight formation.

On Monday, a Tennessee Street Festival was held at Kennedy Center for Al Gore's family, friends, and staff. Most of that day as well as Tuesday were filled with luncheons, receptions, and various galas.

Inauguration day, January 20, dawned sunny and cold. The Gores met the Clintons for a prayer service. At 11:30 A.M. they gathered on the Capitol steps with many thousands in attendance. Supreme Court Justice Thurgood Marshall had been scheduled to swear-in Al Gore, but the justice was too ill. Instead Justice Byron White did the honors. Gore took the same oath to defend the Constitution that he had taken as a representative and as a senator:

> I, Albert Gore, Jr., do solemnly swear that I will support and defend the Constitution of the United States against all enemies foreign and domestic; that I will bear true faith and allegiance to the same; that I take this obligation freely, without any mental reservation or purpose of evasion, and that I will well and faithfully discharge the duties of the office on which I am about to enter."[11]

This time, however, as he swore the oath, it was for a much higher office. As Al Gore, Jr. finished the oath, Bill Clinton grabbed him in an enormous bear hug.

The swearing-in of the President was followed by his short inaugural address. Then the Gores and Clintons went on to a congressional lunch and the inaugural parade. The revelry ended with numerous and glamorous inaugural balls.

With the excitement and celebration over, it was time to go back to work. Clinton and Gore maintained their close working relationship. As George Stephanopoulos, then Clinton communications director noted, "The Vice President goes to almost every meeting the President has and is free to go to any meeting he desires. And before any big decision is made, the President always wants to know: 'What does Al think?'"[12]

Clinton integrated Gore's staff with his own to make for smoother relationships. Gore also influenced numerous appointments, particularly in the areas of the environment and technology. He was responsible for a former legislative aide (who had moved on to become Florida's environmental chief), Carol M. Browner, being appointed to head the EPA. Gore's brother-in-law Frank Hunger took over the Civil Division of the Justice Department.

On March 3, 1993, President Clinton announced the National Performance Review. Every department of the federal government would be examined. The review would be held, "to redesign, to reinvent, to reinvigorate the entire national government."[13] Vice President Al Gore was to be in charge of this huge effort. Gore and his team sought advice from many sources: federal workers, state and local government officials, management experts and the business community. Gore held town meetings with the employees of each cabinet department. Many of these meetings were televised on the cable TV channel C-Span.

On September 7, 1993, Gore appeared with Bill Clinton on the South Lawn of the White House. The Vice President was there to deliver his final report to the President. The men stood in front of two forklifts piled high with government regulations, a symbol of old-fashioned, out-dated government. Gore's report contained 800 recommendations that he estimated would save $108 billion over 5 years, and would cut 252,000 federal jobs by 1998. Some of the changes would require congressional approval, but many could be achieved immediately by presidential executive order. All in all, Gore said that his proposals would—as the title of his report indicated—create a government that works better and costs less.

In the fall of 1993 an important piece of legislation came before Congress. It would create NAFTA (North American Free Trade Agreement). Many people were against this agreement that the Clinton Administration strongly favored. Those opposed argued that U.S. companies would move their manufacturing operations south to Mexico in order to take advantage of cheap Mexican labor. Many U.S. jobs would be lost. The Administration argued that having free trade with Mexico—that is, doing away with tariffs—would cause more export trade and would create more jobs.

One of the principal opponents of the agreement was Ross Perot. He said that we in the United States would hear a giant sucking sound made by jobs rushing to Mexico. Perot's views were influential, and he made them well known at every opportunity. In order to counter Perot's arguments, Al Gore proposed that he debate the issue with Perot on TV. Clinton was enthusiastic about this idea.

Consequently on the CNN talk show *Larry King Live,* on November 9, 1993, Gore and Perot debated the agreement. They also responded to phone call questions from the TV audience for an hour and a half. There was little question of who won the debate. Conservative columnist William Safire's column commenting on the program was headlined, "Gore Flattens Perot."[14] And a Gallup poll scored audience reaction to the debate as almost 2 to 1 for Gore. NAFTA passed, and Al Gore soon left for Mexico to confer with President Carlos

Salinas de Gortari about implementation of the agreement.

Gore also undertook other foreign missions for President Clinton. In mid-December 1993, Gore, Mrs. Gore, and reporters were aboard Air Force Two when it was forced to make an emergency landing in Bishkek, Kyrgyzstan. Gore was on his way to Moscow to arrange for the meeting between President Clinton and Russian President Boris Yeltsin, which was held in January 1994.

In addition Gore took a hand in shaping legislation. He made sure that $1 billion was included in the budget for new technology initiatives. Even while he was still in Congress, he was a strong proponent of the "information superhighway." This in-progress fiber optic link will eventually connect people with sources of education, information, and entertainment.

Gore made certain that the new Service Corps, a way for young Americans to serve their country in return for college tuition grants, had an environmental role. For instance recruits could repair parks or clean up river banks.

Gore has been Bill Clinton's eyes and ears on Capitol Hill. Gore explains his role this way, "As priorities mature on the Hill, the two of us get on the telephone. I serve as a scout to find out where the weak spots are and who needs to be shored up. And then he delivers the *coup de grace.*"[15]

Gore discussed the "information superhighway" with an expert at AT&T Bell Laboratories. Technology that is necessary for the national super computer network is being refined there.

In his inaugural speech in 1961, John F. Kennedy said that the torch of leadership had passed to a new generation. In 1992 the torch was passed to a new generation again. But this last time both the Vice President and the President are part of that new generation. As a team, working together, they are leading the country in a world filled with change.

Chronology

1948—Albert Gore, Jr. is born.

1965—Graduates St. Albans School in Washington, D.C.; enters Harvard University.

1969—Graduates Harvard University; enlists in the U.S. Army.

1970—Marries Mary Elizabeth Aitcheson (known as Tipper) on May 19; ships out for Vietnam on Christmas Day.

1971—Tour of duty ends; enrolls in Vanderbilt University Divinity School; works as a reporter for *The Tennesseean*.

1973—Daughter Karenna is born.

1974—Enters Vanderbilt University Law School

1976—Elected U.S. representative from Fourth District of Tennessee.

1977—Daughter Kristin is born.

1979—Daughter Sarah is born.

1982—Son Albert III is born.

1984—Elected U.S. senator from Tennessee.

1988—Wages unsuccessful campaign for the presidency.

1989—Son Albert III seriously injured; begins writing *Earth In the Balance: Ecology and the Human Spirit.*

1992—Elected United States Vice President.

1993 -1994—Works closely with President Clinton on domestic and foreign policy.

Chapter Notes

Chapter 1

1. Al Gore, "Facing the Crisis of Spirit," in *Vital Speeches of the Day,* August 15, 1992, p. 646.

2. Ibid.

3. Ibid., p 647.

4. Ibid.

Chapter 2

1. *The Tennessean,* April 1, 1948, p. 1.

2. Alex S. Jones, "Al Gore's Double Life," *New York Times Magazine,* October 25, 1992, p. 76.

Chapter 3

1. Hank Hillin, *Al Gore Jr.: His Life and Career* (New York: Birch Lane Press, 1992), p. 31.

2. Alex S. Jones, "Al Gore's Double Life," *New York Times Magazine,* October 25, 1992, p. 44.

3. Hillin, p. 26.

4. Ibid., p. 43.

5. *The Albanian* (Washington, D.C.: St. Albans School Yearbook, 1965), p. 35.

Chapter 4

1. *MacNeil/Lehrer NewsHour,* "The Gore Record," April 13, 1988.

2. Personal interview with John Tyson, April 14, 1993.

3. Ibid.

4. *MacNeil/Lehrer NewsHour,* April 13, 1988.

5. Ibid.

6. Ibid.

7. Hank Hillin, *Al Gore Jr.: His Life and Career* (New York: Birch Lane Press, 1992), p. 70.

Chapter 5

1. *MacNeil/Lehrer NewsHour,* "The Gore Record," April 13, 1988.

2. Hank Hillin, *Al Gore Jr.: His Life and Career* (New York: Birch Lane Press, 1992), p. 78.

3. Ibid.

4. *MacNeil/Lehrer NewsHour,* April 13, 1988.

5. Hillin, p. 78.

6. Ibid., p. 79.

7. Al Gore, *Earth in the Balance: Ecology and the Human Spirit* (New York: Houghton Mifflin Company, 1992), p. 3.

8. SP 5 Albert Gore, Jr., "'Fire Base Blue Is Overrun,'" *The Tennessean,* March 21, 1971, p. 1B.

9. Ibid, p. 2B.

Chapter 6

1. Hank Hillin, *Al Gore Jr.: His Life and Career* (New York: Birch Lane Press, 1992), p. 87.

2. Ibid., pp. 88–89.

3. Ibid., p. 89.

4. Ibid., pp. 89–90.

5. Ibid., p. 89.

6. Ibid., p. 90.

7. Ibid., p. 92.

8. Ibid.

9. Ibid., p. 94.

10. Ibid.

11. Ibid.

12. Ibid., p. 98.

13. Ibid.

Chapter 7

1. Hank Hillin, *Al Gore Jr.: His Life and Career* (New York: Birch Lane Press, 1992), p. 101.

2. "Network Is Proposed For Organ Transplants," *The New York Times,* October 6, 1983, p. A19.

3. David Shribman, "Gores, Father and Son, A Tradition of Activism," *The New York Times,* June 2, 1983, p. B10.

4. Albert Gore, Jr., "The Fork in the Road," *The New Republic,* May 5, 1982, p. 15.

5. Hillin, p. 117.

6. Ibid.

7. Ibid., p. 119.

Chapter 8

1. CQ's Political Staff, *C.Q's Politics in America, 1992, The 102nd Congress* (Washington, D.C.: C.Q Press, 1991), p. 1382.

2. Ibid.

3. Tipper Gore, *Raising PG Kids in an X-rated Society* (Nashville: Abingdon Press, 1987), p. 17.

4. Ibid., p. 19.

5. Ibid., p. 21.

6. Ibid.

7. Ibid., p. 32

8. Ibid., p. 33

9. Hank Hillin, *Al Gore Jr.: His Life and Career* (New York: Birch Lane Press, 1992), p. 3.

10. Ibid.

11. Ibid., p. 136.

Chapter 9

1. *U.S. EPA Oral History Interview-1, William D. Ruckelshaus,* United States Environmental Protection Agency, (Washington, D.C.: January 1993), p. 7.

2. Al Gore, *Earth in the Balance: Ecology and the Human Spirit* (New York: Houghton Mifflin Company, 1992), p. 23.

3. Ibid., p. 19.

4. Ibid., p. 24.

Chapter 10

1. Al Gore, *Earth in the Balance: Ecology and the Human Spirit* (New York: Houghton Mifflin Company, 1992), p. 13.

2. Ibid., p. 14.

3. Michael Kelly, "A Changed Gore, With a Firmer Voice," *The New York Times*, July 21, 1992, p. A15.

4. Ibid.

5. Sandra McElwaine, "Up Close with Tipper Gore," *Good Housekeeping*, March 1993, p. 235.

6. Kelly, p. A15.

7. Gore, p. 2.

8. Ibid., p. 30. ·

9. Ibid., p. 313.

10. Ibid., p. 368.

Chapter 11

1. "Political Briefing Family Affair," *Los Angeles Times*, August 12, 1991, p. A5.

2. "Gore Goes," *The Economist* (London), August 24–30, 1991, p. 24.

3. . . . *talking with David Frost*, September 25, 1992.

4. Sidney Blumenthal, "Perotnoia," *The New Republic*, June 15, 1992, pp. 26–27.

5. "Excerpts From Clinton's and Gore's Remarks on the Ticket," *The New York Times*, July 10, 1992, p. A16.

6. Ibid.

7. Gwen Ifill, "Clinton Selects Senator Gore to Be His Running Mate," *The New York Times*, July 10, 1992, p. A16.

Chapter 12

1. Bill Clinton, "Acceptance Address," *Vital Speeches of the Day*, August 15, 1992, p. 642.

2. Howard G. Chua-eoan, "First Friends," *People Weekly*, November 16, 1992, pp. 95–97.

3. *Facts on File*, Vol. 52, No. 2698 (August 13, 1992), p. 586.

4. R.W. Apple, Jr., "Quayle on the Offensive: Vice President Comes Out Hitting Clinton, But Gore Holds His Own on the Main Issues," *The New York Times*, October 14, 1992, p. A1.

5. Ibid.

6. *Facts on File*, Vol. 52, No. 2711 (November 5, 1992), p. 829.

7. Sam Fulwood, III, "Gore Adds Personal Touch in Campaign's Final Days," *Los Angeles Times*, November 3, 1992, p. A12.

8. Ibid.

9. Kent Jenkins, Jr., "2ND Fiddle From Tennessee: How Will Gore Play?," *The Washington Post*, January 20, 1993, p. F4.

10. Ibid.

11. Oath of office taken by Vice President Albert Gore, Jr., January 20, 1993 in Washington, D.C.

12. Jack Nelson, "Gore May Emerge as Most Influential Vice President," *Los Angeles Times*, March 15, 1993, p. A14.

13. Al Gore, *From Red Tape to Results: Creating a Government that Works Better and Costs Less*, Report of the National Performance Review (Washington, D.C.: September 7, 1993), preface.

14. William Safire, "Gore Flattens Perot," *The New York Times*, November 11, 1993, p. A27.

15. Nelson, p. A14.

Further Reading

Gore, Al. *Earth in the Balance: Ecology and the Human Spirit.* New York: Houghton Mifflin Co., 1992.

Gore, Tipper, *Raising PG Kids in an X-rated Society.* Nashville, Tenn.: Abingdon Press, 1987.

Hillen, Hank. *Al Gore, Jr.: His Life and Career.* New York: Birch Lane Press, 1992.

Middleton, Nick. *Atlas of Environmental Issues.* Oxford, England: Ilex Publishers, Ltd., 1989.

Newsweek Magazine. "Saving the Earth," *Newsweek Just For Kids,* March 29, 1993.

Index